Approved by LEO

The finest seal of approval based on taste, looks and durability. All done by my son Leo at 1,5 years old.

I0163242

ISBN

ISBN-13: 978-91-980904-7-5

CONTACT INFO

Skyborn Works, Lyckselevagen 38, LGH 1102.
162 67 Vallingby. SWEDEN.
T: +46 73 649 83 11
contact@skybornworks.com

www.futurelittle.com
www.skybornworks.com

REBEL
FLAG

CAMOFLAGE CLOTHING

COWBOY HAT & BOOTS

TRUCKER HAT

BELT
BUCKLE

PICKUP TRUCK

AIRBOAT

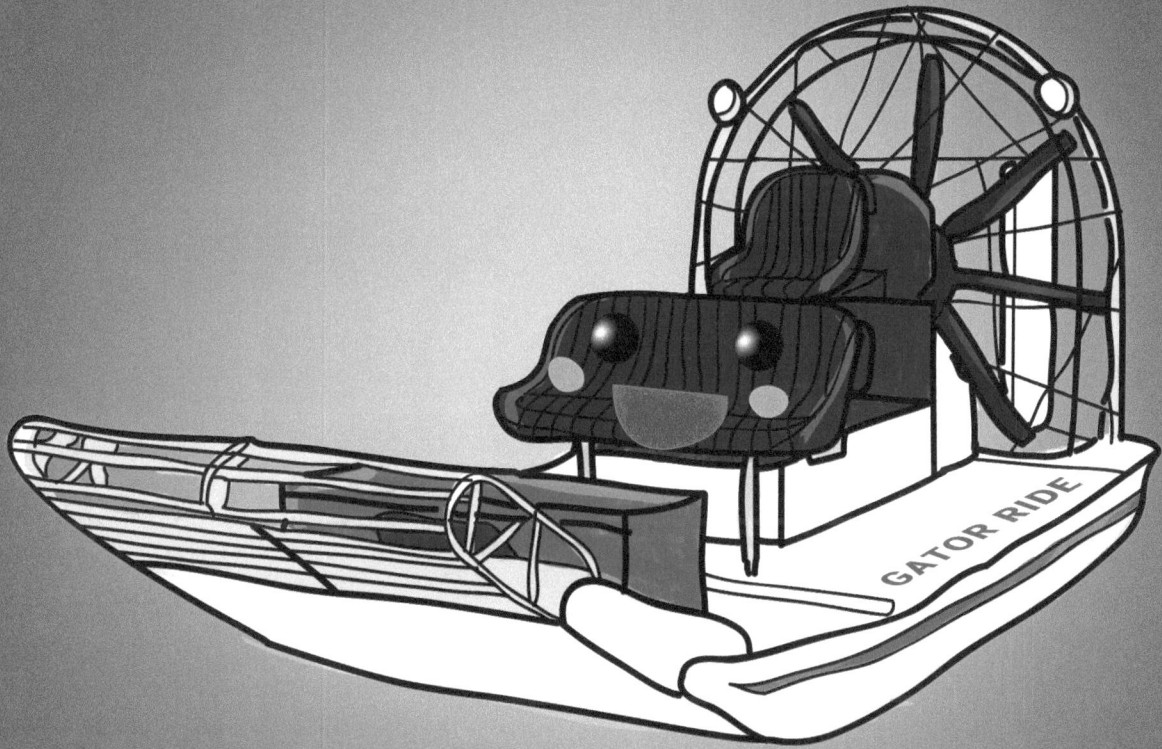

TRAILER

RUSTY FARM EQUIPMENT

BARBECUE GRILL

SHOTGUN

BANJO

COUNTRY MUSIC

NASCAR
RACING

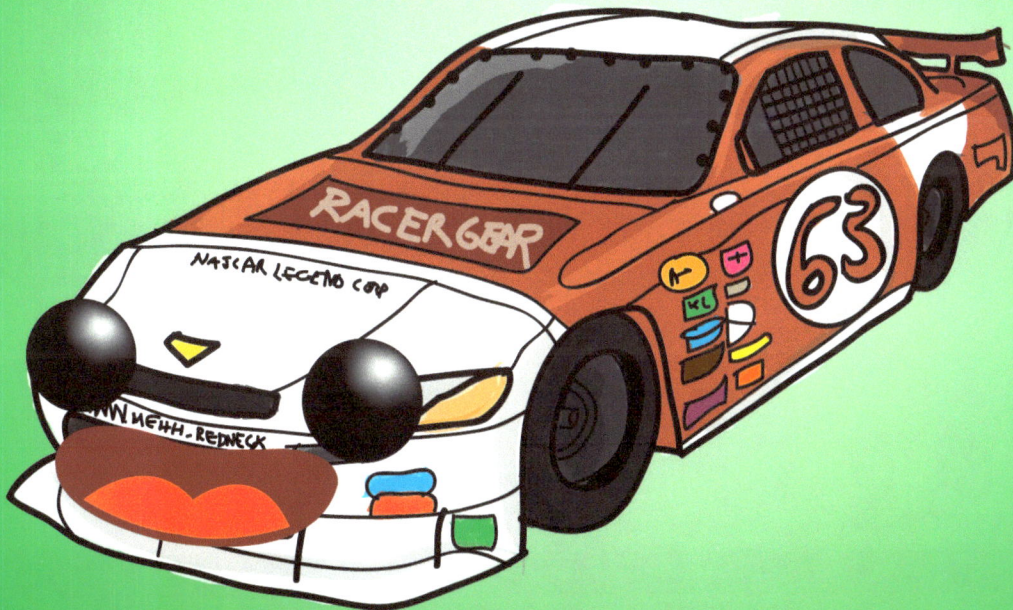

HUNTING

ALLIGATOR FISHING

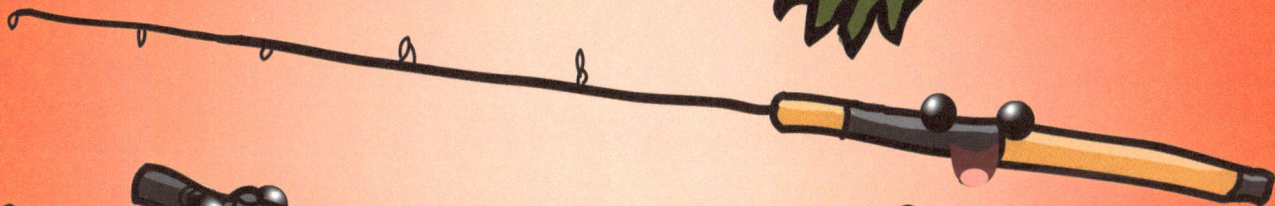

MOONSHINING

MUDDING

FRIED FOOD

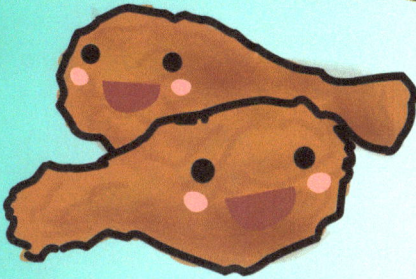

BEANS & CORNBREAD

ROADKILL DISH

WAFFLE RESTAURANT

www.ingramcontent.com/pod-product-compliance
Lightning Source LLC
Chambersburg PA
CBHW042100040426
42448CB00002B/76

9789198090475